DATE DUE			

Our Endangered Planet
SOIL

Suzanne Winckler
and
Mary M. Rodgers

LERNER PUBLICATIONS COMPANY • MINNEAPOLIS

Thanks to Jeffrey J. Schmidt, Cindy Hartmon, Zachary Marell, and Gary Hansen for their help in preparing this book.

Words in **bold** type are listed in a glossary that starts on page 67.

LIBRARY OF CONGRESS CATALOGING-IN-PUBLICATION DATA

Winckler, Suzanne, 1946–
    Our endangered planet. Soil / Suzanne Winckler and Mary M. Rodgers.
      p. cm.
    Includes bibliographical references and index.
    Summary: Discusses the formation and the role of different types of soils and how they have been endangered through unwise farming, mining, and grazing.
    ISBN 0-8225-2508-9 (lib. bdg.)
    1. Soils—Juvenile literature. 2. Soil degradation—Juvenile literatuare.
3. Soil conservation—Juvenile literature. 4. Agriculture—Juvenile literatuare. [1. Soils. 2. Soil degradation. 3. Soil conservation.
4. Agriculture.] I. Rodgers, Mary M. (Mary Madeline), 1954– . II. Title.
S591.3.W56 1993
631.4—dc20
                                    92–39902
                                    CIP
                                    AC

Manufactured in the United States of America

1 2 3 4 5 6 – I/JR – 99 98 97 96 95 94

Front cover: A farmer grabs a handful of fertile soil in the central United States. Back cover: (Left) On the Mediterranean island of Cyprus, an artist shapes a pot from clay soil. (Right) To build irrigation canals, developers have cut down portions of the tropical rain forests of Guyana in South America. The exposed soil, which is too poor to nourish food crops, can be easily washed away by the area's heavy rainfall.

Recycled paper

Recyclable

CONTENTS

OUR ENDANGERED PLANET

In the 1960s, astronauts first traveled beyond the earth's protective atmosphere and were able to look back at our planet. What they saw was a beautiful globe, turning slowly in space. That image reminds us that our home planet has limits, for we know of no other place that can support life.

The various parts of our natural environment—including air, water, soil, plants, and animals—are partners in making our planet a good place to live. If we endanger one element, the other partners are badly affected, too.

People throughout the world are working to protect and heal the earth's environment. They recognize that making nature our ally and not our victim is the way to shape a common future. Because we have only one planet to share, its health and survival mean that we all can live.

Soil may be the forgotten partner in our planet's complex environment. But without healthy soil, no living thing on our planet could survive. Most of the foods we eat either come from or depend on the soil. We dig up the soil to find valuable fuels and minerals.

As our planet's human population has increased, we have looked for ways to grow more food. Some of these methods use too many chemicals, which damage the soil. As we have expanded our cities, we have cut down plants whose roots hold the soil in place. To locate precious minerals, we have scarred the land and have failed to return it to its former condition.

Scientists, builders, and farmers have come up with new ways for us to reduce our impact on the soil. As buyers of food, we can support farming practices that protect the soil. As home gardeners, we can preserve the soil in our own backyards. As students, we can help other people to learn about the importance of healthy soil in the global environment.

CHAPTER ONE

LIFE BENEATH OUR FEET

Nearly half of the world's 5.4 billion people live in cities. Few urban folk grow their own vegetables, raise their own meat, or make their own houses with lumber or bricks. In cities, people buy these products from other people.

As a result, we often forget that our vegetables, fruits, eggs, meat, lumber, and building materials all begin with the soil. Fruit trees and vegetables need soil to survive, and the plants eaten by livestock grow in soil. We get lumber from trees. Mud and straw are the raw materials for some kinds of bricks.

(Left) Market stalls in Lausanne, Switzerland, display a variety of foods grown in and near this mountainous European country. (Right) A young Peruvian paints a small bead made of hardened clay soil.

Earthworms live in moist, warm soil and feed on dead plants. By crawling and pushing through the soil in search of food and air, earthworms help to loosen and mix decaying matter. If there is not enough air under the ground, earthworms come to the surface, where fans of fishing collect them as bait.

Soil covers our planet like a layer of skin. The thinnest—and most fertile—part of the layer, called **topsoil**, averages only 5 to 7 inches (12 to 18 centimeters) thick. In this narrow band, we grow most of the foods we eat.

Although it is not a living substance, soil is home to billions of **organisms** (life forms). Some, like ants, beetles, and earthworms, we can easily see. Others, called **microorganisms**, are too small for us to view without a microscope. They include many kinds of fungi and **bacteria**, as well as tiny animals that help to break down plant and animal remains in the soil. A pinch of soil might contain millions of microorganisms.

NAKED MOLE-RATS
The Soil's Hairless Wonders

Naked mole-rats, despite their name, are not naked, nor are they moles or rats. These small, hairless creatures, which belong to the rodent family, live completely underground in colonies of up to 100 animals. They use their large buckteeth to dig a complex system of tunnels in the clay soil of the east African nations of Kenya, Somalia, and Ethiopia.

The leader of a society of naked mole-rats is the queen, who produces all the babies with the help of a few breeding males. Other members of the colony dig tunnels, find food, or protect the group from harm. Young naked mole-rats become part of the colony's work force within a few months of their birth.

Naked mole-rats feed on yams and other plants whose nourishing roots cross the paths of the tunnels. East African farmers consider the animal a pest because it chews on the roots of their crops, but the feeding habits of naked mole-rats rarely destroy plants. In fact, the presence of naked mole-rats—which only live in hard, dry clay soil—gives scientists clues about the type of soil they are studying.

A naked mole-rat chews on an underground root using its large, curved teeth.

LIKE A ROCK

Our planet has lots of kinds of soil. A handful of soil from your backyard is not the same as a handful taken from a faraway forest, hillside, riverbank, or beach. Some soils crumble like cake, others are sticky like glue. Still others feel sandy, and some feel gritty. Some soils are black, others are gray, and still others are red or yellow. Why are there so many kinds?

That handful of soil from your backyard was once hard rock. Our planet has many types of rock, including limestone, granite, basalt, slate, and marble. Each kind of rock serves as the main ingredient, or **parent material**, for a specific type of soil. Now let's look at how rock becomes soil.

Over a long, long time, the parent material weathers, or slowly changes, because of physical or chemical actions. **Physical weathering** results from the forces of sun, wind, and water on rock. In coastal areas of the world, for example, the constant impact of waves crashing against rocks causes them to break and crack. As the waves continue to pound, the pieces

There are many kinds of soil on our planet, including a rich, dark type (above) that is ideal for farming and a gritty variety (below) whose yellow color comes from iron.

Wearing wet suits, boys dodge incoming ocean waves. The force of the water breaks up nearby rocks into smaller and smaller pieces that will eventually become sand.

of rock become smaller and smaller until they are particles of soil.

Soil is also formed when water seeps into cracks in a rock and rubs against the rock's surfaces. In cold areas, this water freezes and expands. The resulting ice works like a lever, prying the rock into pieces.

Direct sunlight can also heat and swell rocks. At night, the rocks cool and decrease in size. Over a long period, the strain of constantly expanding and contracting makes the rocks crumble.

Chunks of basalt—a hard, dark volcanic rock— line the coast of Senegal in West Africa. A very common material, basalt has even been found on the moon.

(Far left) The chemicals and other elements in soil are clearly visible in this exposed rock on the continent of Antarctica. The bright green color may mean that the rock contains copper ore. (Left) Wind and rain can carry soil particles into rivers, turning the waterways muddy and brown. Here, a woman watches the Nile River, which flows through several countries in Africa.

Chemical weathering occurs when chemical elements in the soil—such as carbon, oxygen, hydrogen, calcium, and iron—mix with and change one another. Water, which is composed of hydrogen and oxygen, is a powerful dissolving agent. It is also a major force in the different reactions that take place during chemical weathering. For example, when carbon, oxygen, and water come together in soil, they form carbonic acid. Carbonic acid is one of the compounds that eats away at rock to make soil.

Physical and chemical weathering both help to create soil, but climate also has a role. In cold, dry climates, where rocks expand and contract day and night, physical weathering is the main way of making soil.

In warm, wet climates, chemical weathering is more important because rainwater mixes with other elements to create chemical compounds that break down the parent material.

SOIL MOVEMENTS

Wind and water play important roles in moving soils from one place to another. **Loess** is windblown soil that originally lay under ancient glaciers (slow-moving masses of ice). **Alluvium** is soil carried by fast-flowing rivers from mountains to lowlands. Loess and alluvium are very fertile soils that contain large amounts of the **nutrients** (foods) that plants need to grow.

The grain-producing areas of North America, Europe, and Asia owe their plentiful harvests to loess. The alluvial soils of the Tigris and Euphrates Valley in Iraq, of the Mississippi Delta in the United States, and of the Mekong Delta in Vietnam are also prime farmland.

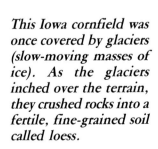

This Iowa cornfield was once covered by glaciers (slow-moving masses of ice). As the glaciers inched over the terrain, they crushed rocks into a fertile, fine-grained soil called loess.

MAKING SOIL A SCIENCE

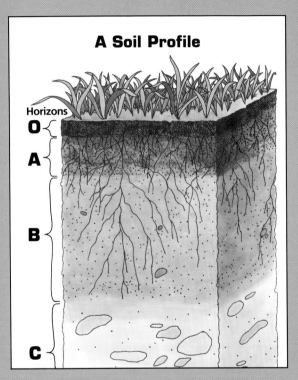

A Soil Profile

Horizons

O
A
B
C

The diagram shows a soil profile from a site where the soil is old and has not been disturbed. The shallowest horizon—marked "O"—is the organic level, where once-living materials are rotting. Horizon "A" is topsoil. The deepest horizons, marked "B" and "C," are the subsoil (where weathering is taking place) and the parent material.

Unlike math or astronomy, the study of soil—called pedology—is a young science. It was not until the late 1700s that scientists in Europe began to examine the effects of soil weathering. They also researched nutrients in the soil and linked different rocks to the making of different soils.

In the late 1800s, a Russian natural scientist named Vasily V. Dokuchayev put together a soil theory (an unproved explanation of facts). Dokuchayev outlined the soil's development from layers of rock at the earth's surface. He also noted that the actions of tiny life forms and of climate change these layers and affect soil fertility.

Dokuchayev and other scientists in Europe and the United States expanded pedology to include the physical makeup of soils, their distribution throughout our planet, and their management. A branch of this science focuses on the arrangement of layers, called horizons, in a soil profile. The profile—which can be drawn as if a slice were taken out of the ground—shows how deep the layers are in a particular place. These areas of pedology are based on the work of early pioneers in the study of the soil.

A RECIPE FOR SOIL

No matter what the parent material, all soils are made of four basic ingredients—**minerals, organic matter,** air, and water. Minerals can be ground-up rocks or other nonliving substances. Some of these substances—such as nitrogen, phosphorus, and potassium—help plants to grow. Soil scientists use the size of mineral particles to classify soils as either sand, silt, or clay.

Sand particles are large enough for us to see with the naked eye. If you looked at just a pinch of sand, you would see that each particle looks like a very small rock. Sand particles do not usually stick together, and they feel gritty.

Smaller than sand, silt particles are powdery, and you would need a microscope or a magnifying glass to see them. Clay has the smallest mineral particles, which are shiny and sticky when wet. When dry, they form clods that are almost as hard as bricks. The smallest clay particles can only be viewed with a powerful instrument called an electron microscope.

Soil particles vary in size. Individual bits of sand (top) *look like tiny rocks. Clay particles* (above), *however, are packed so close together that we cannot see them without a powerful microscope.*

(Left) A soil scientist uses a long tube to take a core sample. By pushing the tube into the ground, experts can examine soil near the surface as well as at deeper levels. (Below) Most soils are a combination of many kinds of particles.

Most soils contain a mixture of sand, silt, and clay. By looking at and feeling the soil, a scientist can determine its texture—that is, how much sand, silt, or clay the soil contains. A soil's texture tells us how well it passes nutrients to plants. Sandy soil is a very poor supplier of nutrients, because nutrients and water can run quickly through and out of the sand's large particles. Loam—a specific mixture of sand, silt, and clay—holds enough water and nutrients for roots to grow in it.

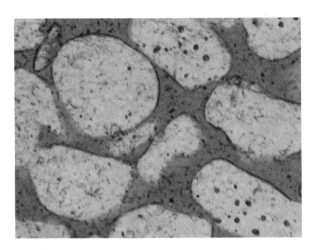

Photographed at 46 times its actual size, this piece of sandstone shows the large spaces, or pores, that exist between soil particles. Most sandstone is formed of particles that water has moved from their original site to a new location.

A center pivot irrigator pumps up water that lies deep in the ground, spraying it in a wide, circular curve.

CHANGE PARTNERS

Soil is part solid, part liquid, and part gas. We have discussed the solid portion—the mixture of mineral particles and organic matter. Now let's look at the liquid and gas components. If you filled a large glass bowl with rocks of many different sizes, you would notice that there are spaces between the rocks. If you put water in the bowl, the water would fill most of the spaces.

Spreading through soil is a network of spaces called **pores** that are filled with water and air—the liquid and gas partners of soil. Air and water come from the earth's atmosphere and are constantly changing places with one another in the pores of the soil.

When water is taken up by the roots of a plant or when it evaporates (changes back to a gas and reenters the atmosphere), the empty space is filled by air. Then, when rains come, the water filters down through the pores in the soil and pushes out the air. This water trapped in the soil is called **groundwater.**

A MAJOR BREAKDOWN

Most living things, after they die, are likely to become part of the soil's organic matter. The dead plants and animals form the diet of billions of earthworms, bacteria, and microorganisms. As these tiny creatures feed, they break down fallen leaves, rotting fruit, and dead animals, mixing these and other materials into the soil.

The process of breaking down dead materials is called **decomposition**. The work of microorganisms is never done, because plants and animals are constantly dying. For this reason, soils contain organic matter in all stages of decomposition.

Over time, decaying vegetation can become packed down in swamps and marshes. The result is peat, a spongy material that people in Ireland cut and dry and then burn as a low-cost fuel.

Sparse scrub vegetation grows in the Sahel, a semi-desert region that spans the African continent.

Prairies contain many plants, including grasses, forbs (herbs that are not grass), and flowers. These various species (kinds) pass their nutrients and organic matter to the rich soil and provide food for animals that are native to the prairie.

Plants and animals that are completely decomposed (rotted) create a nutrient-rich material called **humus**. Organic matter—especially humus—is important to plant growth and helps the soil to hold its moisture. But not all soils have equal amounts of organic matter. Deserts, for example, nourish only a few kinds of plants, so desert soils contain very little organic matter. By comparison, prairies support dense stands of grass that practically become humus factories.

CHAPTER TWO

TREATING THE SOIL LIKE DIRT

About 10,000 years ago, our ancestors figured out how to use soil and seeds to grow food. This discovery was the beginning of farming. Early farmers also tamed wild animals—such as cows, pigs, sheep, and goats—and raised them for their fur, bones, meat, and milk. The animals fed on grasses and other plants.

Farming sharply changed human culture by giving people a reason to settle down and live together in villages. Farming also made life easier. People no longer had to wander long distances in search of food.

(Left) A small plane sprays yellow chemicals on a field in Arkansas to kill unwanted insects and other pests.

But farming also changed the appearance of our planet. Villages, towns, cities, and cultivated fields came to dominate many areas of the world. In the last 10,000 years, we have found many ways to feed and shelter our families and an ever-growing global population.

In many countries, each farm still provides food for only the family that lives on it. In other places, huge estates are planted with crops that are bought and sold around the world. As the earth's population has increased, so has the need to expand the amount of land devoted to farming.

In recent decades, to feed greater numbers of people, we have plowed new fields and have even planted in some soils that can barely support life. We have continued to cut down forests and other vegetation to create more farmland.

These actions expose the soil to many hazards. Without trees and plants to anchor the soil, it can be washed off hillsides by rain. Winds can blow loose soil into rivers, lakes, and oceans. Some farming practices—although designed to grow more food—take away the soil's minerals.

All of these changes have weakened the soil's ability to nourish us. Let's look at some specific ways that the soil has become endangered.

GETTING CARRIED AWAY

Erosion, the wearing away of topsoil by wind and water, strips away the earth's thin, protective layer. Of all the events altering the world's soils, erosion is the most widespread and serious. Globally, 124 million acres (50 million hectares) of our planet's farmable land are lost to erosion every year. This amount nearly equals a territory the size Spain!

Water and wind move topsoil far away from its original home. The redeposited soil may block the flow of a river or stream.

As they pass over the land, floodwaters carry valuable topsoil into rivers.

On flat land, erosion takes away nutrient-rich topsoil from cropland. As a result, the roots of the crops cannot reach enough soil nutrients to grow.

Many events—some natural, some people-made—cause erosion. The natural pulling motion of ocean waves, for example, can eat away at a shoreline. Although erosion occurs naturally, people have sped up the process over recent decades.

We cause erosion by taking away the protective covering of trees, shrubs, grasses, and other plants that safeguard the soil. Construction companies that clear ground to build roads, houses, or shopping malls can expose soil to erosion by wind and water. Logging practices, such as clear-cutting (the removal of all the trees in a forest), leave the soil with nothing to cling to, so it easily blows or washes away.

Strong winds can blow topsoil from cropland.

Rivers have brought so much sediment-laden water to Bangladesh, a low country in southern Asia, that people have set up barriers to control the sludge.

Erosion can be especially severe in hilly or mountainous places that have been cleared of trees and other vegetation. As rainfall rushes down the bare slopes, the water picks up loose soil particles and carries them to lower elevations. Treeless hillsides in the Himalaya Mountains of southern Asia have allowed rainwater to bring huge amounts of loose soil to the Bay of Bengal. The deposits are so large that a new island may soon appear above the bay's surface.

One of the results of erosion is **sedimentation,** the gradual buildup of soils at a new location. Because rivers often carry sediment, their mouths (places where rivers empty into larger bodies of water) may be heavily sedimented. Sedimentation has changed the Mississippi River in the United States, for example. It flows southward from Minnesota to the Gulf of Mexico. Estimates predict that sedimentation has extended the river's mouth outward about 75 miles (121 kilometers) from where it was a century ago.

Sedimentation has many other damaging effects. Harbors that are full of sediment must be dredged or ships cannot use them. Rivers with too much sediment hold less floodwater and can eventually overflow. Plants and animals that inhabit rivers and lakes often die when the water they live in is made shallower by heavy sedimentation.

The equipment on a dredging boat sucks up and removes sediment from Biscayne Bay in southern Florida. Dredging deepens the bay so that large ships, such as naval vessels and ocean liners, can dock at the port of Miami.

POISONED SOIL

Every day, we use chemicals to make our lives easier. We put them on our lawns to kill weeds. We clean machinery, appliances, and floors with them. We pump chemicals into cars and trucks to make them run. Some factories also use chemicals to manufacture goods.

After the manufacturing process is over, leftover chemicals—called by-products—are collected and put in barrels. But what happens to these used or unwanted chemicals? Sometimes they are dumped or buried in the ground, where they can contaminate water and soil. Because they endanger life, these chemicals are called hazardous wastes, and disposing of them is a major environmental problem.

Big companies create more chemical by-products than households do, but families and businesses are struggling with the disposal of hazardous wastes. One organization in particular—the U.S. Department of Defense— faces the challenge on a large scale. Two large military sites, the Rocky Mountain Arsenal in Colorado and the Hanford Nuclear Reservation in Washington State, buried their hazardous wastes in poorly protected pits.

The barrels rotted and eventually leaked their contents into the soil. Before the Department of Defense can allow people to live on these parcels of land, it must clean up the hazardous wastes—a job that could take as long as 30 years.

Kids in Utah are involved in hazardous-waste cleanup, too. During a discussion in a sixth-grade classroom, students looked at a map of waste sites in Salt Lake City. One of the sites was near their school—a spot the students called ''that old barrel yard.'' After many months of calling officials and writing letters, the sixth graders talked to the city's mayor, who agreed to get the mess cleaned up within 18 months.

The students didn't stop with this success, however. They pressed their state legislators—again through phone calls, letters, and visits—to set up a cleanup fund just for Utah's hazardous-waste sites. All of the legislators voted for the proposed law. As one of the students said, ''big things can happen in small steps.''

Fully protected by special clothing, a clean-up crew uncovers rotted barrels at the Hanford Nuclear Reservation in Washington State.

IRRIGATION'S IMPACT

In dry regions of the world, farmers bring water from nearby lakes, rivers, or wells to nourish their crops. Farmers sometimes dig canals to route water from streams to fields. In recent times, inventors have designed huge sprinklers that spray water on crops.

No matter what the method, **irrigation**—the artificial watering of crops—gives farmers more control over their harvest. Instead of depending on annual flooding or rainy weather, which can be unpredictable, farmers can choose when to irrigate and how much water to use. Through irrigation, farmers have been able to grow more food. In fact, about 15 percent of the world's farmland is irrigated, and these lands produce more than 30 percent of the world's crops.

(Left) **A Saudi Arabian farmer checks the pipes that slowly drip water to his cornfield.** *(Above)* **In the central United States, huge sprinklers irrigate crops.**

Too much irrigation without proper drainage has pushed dissolved salts to the surface of the land in northern Pakistan. Because most crops cannot survive in salty soil, farming has suffered in several sections of this southern Asian nation.

But irrigation has its disadvantages, too. In some cases, using too much water will force nutrients deep into the soil, robbing shallow plant roots of the foods they need to grow. This action, called **leaching,** often happens to sandy soils in areas of high rainfall or heavy irrigation.

All irrigation water contains dissolved salts that eventually build up in the soil and cause plants to wilt. Unless the salts are successfully leached below the root zone, they can damage farmland. In some cases, high amounts of irrigation water push the salt to the surface of the soil. Thick, salty crusts on farmland in Pakistan, Australia, Ethiopia, Sudan, and Egypt make the soil unfit for growing crops. Experts suggest that 11 percent of Africa's farmable land has been damaged by **salination** (salt buildup).

WORN OUT

Intensive farming—plowing and planting the same crop in the same field every year—can wear out the soil by using up its precious nutrients. Eventually, crops stop growing in the field because the soil lacks enough essential foods to nourish the plants.

Thousands of years ago, when farmers wore out a plot of land, they abandoned it and moved to new ground. In modern times, new farmland is not only expensive, it is also in short supply. If a plot starts to lose its nutrients, farmers add chemicals, called **fertilizers,** to the soil. Although fertilizers help plants to grow, they do not replace the soil's nutrients. In poor soils, farmers usually apply fertilizers every year.

Modern farmers rely on other chemicals, too. **Insecticides** kill unwanted insects and worms that eat crops. **Herbicides** destroy weeds that compete with crops for water and nutrients. Both of these chemicals are **pesticides.**

Wearing a mask, a Senegalese worker sprays insecticides on a field to get rid of tsetse flies.

(Above) *By applying agricultural chemicals, farmers in Australia are able to produce huge harvests of wheat. (Right) Piles of empty containers reflect the widespread use of fertilizers and pesticides on U.S. farms.*

Fertilizers, insecticides, and herbicides allow farmers to produce abundant crops even on nutrient-poor land. Unwise use of farm chemicals, however, harms the soil, the groundwater, and the surface water. The unneeded or overused chemicals seep into the ground, polluting the water and killing beneficial microorganisms in the soil.

Some chemicals flow from land into rivers and lakes. The chemicals can then poison the water or change its chemistry

Strip miners in Zaire, a nation in central Africa, shovel tin-laden soil onto a conveyor belt.

so that plants and animals cannot live there anymore.

SCARRED FOR LIFE

Many of the world's valuable minerals are found in rocks near the earth's surface. To reach these minerals—which include coal, phosphate, oil shale, and tar sands—workers strip away the upper layers of soil in a method known as **strip mining.** Powerful, motor-driven shovels remove the soil to uncover the minerals, which are then broken up and loaded onto trucks.

In the past, strip miners in Canada, the United States, and Europe cleared the vegetation and dug up the soil to reach the minerals. These actions often led to erosion and mudslides. After the minerals were gone, the mines were abandoned. Canada alone has more than 100,000 acres (40,470 hectares) of land harmed by strip mining.

Laws now force some U.S., Canadian, and European strip-mining companies to restore the land. Miners collect the soil in piles, take out the minerals, and return the soil to its previous location. Even when done this way, strip mining disturbs the soil's structure, which needs time to return to its original condition.

In Kentucky, wildcatters (people who mine in secret to avoid environmental protection laws) bulldoze the soil to uncover coal deposits (above). After removing the coal, the wildcatters abandon the site. Laws in Kentucky require mining companies to restore the land after their operations have ended. After replacing the soil, many firms plant trees, flowers, and other vegetation (right) to prevent erosion and mudslides.

CHAPTER THREE

REAPING WHAT WE'VE SOWN

The soil keeps no secrets. An airplane's view of our planet reveals areas where erosion, sedimentation, and salination have damaged the soil. One of the ways we can change what is happening to the soil is to learn from our mistakes. Let's look at some specific examples of soil problems—and their consequences—in several parts of the world.

THE DUST BOWL

In the 1930s, the Great Plains of the central United States were experiencing a

(Left) **In 1936, a farmer and his two children ran for cover during a blinding dust storm in Oklahoma.**

drought—a period when it does not rain for a very long time. For an area that needs rain to raise crops, a drought can be a disaster.

Although droughts are a natural part of life on the Great Plains, this dry spell was different. Farmers had plowed up and killed the deep-rooted prairie grasses, which knitted the soil together. In place of these grasses, the farmers planted grain crops with shallow roots. Each fall, they harvested the ripe grains. Over the winter, until crops grew again, the farmers left the soil with no protective covering.

When high winds whipped across the Great Plains, they lifted up the fertile topsoil in great clouds of dust and carried it far away. Scientists found soil particles in the eastern United States that had originated in New Mexico—a distance of

2,000 miles (3,219 kilometers)! Day turned to night as the skies were blackened with airborne soil.

Without rain and the fertile topsoil, crops in the Great Plains could not grow. By the late 1930s, the storms and drought had damaged about 50 million acres (20 million hectares) of farmland—an area as big as the state of Nebraska. Farmers could not earn a living, and many of them abandoned their homes in Colorado, New Mexico, Oklahoma, Kansas, and Texas for a new life in California. The disaster caused the U.S. government to set up the Soil Conservation Service to teach farmers how to protect their land.

Oklahoma's farmers now work with officials of the Soil Conservation Service to learn how to use water resources and soil wisely.

An old Egyptian artwork shows some of the farming practices that produced crops in ancient times.

EGYPT'S NILE RIVER

The Nile—the longest river on earth—stretches for 4,145 miles (6,671 kilometers) on the African continent before emptying into the Mediterranean Sea. Each year, the Nile floods its banks and deposits huge amounts of soil in Egypt, a desert country of 55 million people. The soil forms a fertile **floodplain**—an area near the riverbanks that consists of layers of river-carried sediment. Five thousand years ago, Egyp-

tian farmers irrigated the nutrient-rich soils of the Nile's floodplain. Modern farmers are continuing this practice.

Because they depend on the annual flooding of the Nile, Egyptians have tried to control this important event with dams. The dams direct the flooding and store water for irrigating crops. Working like backstops on baseball fields, dams keep water and sediment from moving toward the Nile's mouth.

But the dams in Egypt also trap almost all the fertile soil carried by the Nile River. Without new deposits of soil, Egyptian farmers must use chemical fertilizers to grow their crops. The farmers can no longer simply depend on nature's cycle of flooding and soil depositing.

The Aswan High Dam (below) has controlled flooding and has limited the access of modern Egyptian farmers to the waters of the Nile River. Before the dam was built, annual flooding spread new, nutrient-rich soil on farming plots near the riverbank. To replace lost nutrients, many farmers now spray their crops with chemicals (left).

Some species of acacia trees, especially those that grow in Australia, have developed a high tolerance for salty soil.

SALTY SOILS IN AUSTRALIA

About a hundred years ago, farmers in Australia began to cut down thick stands of deep-rooted eucalyptus and acacia trees that lined Australia's seacoasts. In place of the trees, the farmers planted lush grasses as pasture for livestock. Eventually, herders noticed patches of salty soil in their fields where nothing would grow. Scientists discovered that the salt in the soil came from salt-bearing mists that constantly blew inland on Pacific breezes.

Before farmers removed the eucalyptus and acacia forests, much of the salty mist landed on the trees, which can stand the salt. Rainfall and irrigation water had leached the rest of the salt from the topsoil and carried it deep into the ground. Without the protective covering of native trees and shrubs, however, much more salt gathered underground. As it eventually

rose to the surface, it formed crusty, barren patches in the topsoil.

SOILS THAT TRICK THE EYE

The Amazon Basin, a huge area in South America, includes rivers and streams that flow into the Amazon River. The region, which holds one-third of the world's tropical rain forests, experiences powerful and frequent tropical downpours. The showers pelt the treetops with as much as 200 inches (508 centimeters) of rain per year.

Because tropical forests look so lush, people have assumed that tropical soils must also be very fertile. Farmers and developers cut down these forests to grow food crops and to plant grass for livestock. But soon after the forests are removed, the soils reveal how poor they are. In fact, the soils in the Amazon Basin are the worst soils in the world. They are thin, have few nutrients, and cannot support many crops.

Scientists have found that most of the nutrients in the rain forest are in the **debris**—the fallen leaves, fruits, and

The eastern section of Ecuador, a small South American nation, is part of the Amazon Basin and holds large tropical rain forests. To produce food for their families, the region's farmers have cut down rain-forest plants and have sown seeds in the nutrient-poor soil.

branches lying on the forest floor. Rainforest plants have special roots that take up nutrients from the debris. Some roots feed on the nutrients in water that flows down the bark of trees. When developers and farmers clear a rain forest, they expose the thin soil to heavy rains that cause erosion, flooding, and mudslides. The result is a barren landscape that is unable to support crops, livestock, or trees.

Dying vegetation that lines the forest floor nourishes the tall, wide buttress roots of a tropical tree.

A herder in Mali, West Africa, is surrounded by his flock of sheep. Grazing too many animals on too little land has damaged the soil in much of this area of the continent.

SAHELIAN NIGHTMARE

The Sahel is a broad area of central Africa south of the Sahara Desert. Since the 1970s, the Sahel has seen desert conditions expand southward because of a process called **desertification.** Barren sand now covers huge pieces of once-farmable land in Senegal, Mauritania, Mali, Niger, Burkina Faso, and Chad.

The expanding desert is largely a people-made soil problem. At the same time as the Sahara has been expanding, the populations of the Sahel have also increased at a rapid rate. Having more people to feed means raising more livestock and growing more crops for food.

Overgrazing of livestock—putting too many animals in a field to eat grass—strips the field down to the topsoil. Overplanting usually means farming land again and again whose soil has become too poor to nourish many crops. Eventually, the land is abandoned. Having more people to feed also increases the demand for wood to be used as cooking fuel. In the Sahel, trees are cut down or stripped of their branches, leaving nothing to protect the soil from erosion.

In Morocco, North Africa, workers have planted palm and tamarisk trees to prevent blowing sand from harming valuable cropland.

CHAPTER FOUR

THE NEW FARMERS

When we mistreat the soil, it stops working for us. If we change the elements that create and enrich soil, we harm the soil itself. Some of the people who understand this best are farmers. They know that, although soil requires hundreds and often thousands of years to be made, it can be lost or poisoned in only a few seasons. Without healthy soil, farmers cannot grow healthy crops.

Young and old farmers around the world are learning that they must take care of the soil. They are experimenting with new agricultural methods. This new kind of farming is called **sustainable agriculture.** It involves all aspects of farming, from how farmers till (plow) their soil to how they choose which crops to grow. But the main rule of sustainable agriculture is simple—protect the soil!

(Left) An aerial view of fields in Utah shows the shapes made by strip cropping, a farming practice that reduces erosion and sedimentation. (Above) In Myanmar (formerly Burma), a worker waters jasmine plants, which produce flowers that are popular in this Southeast Asian country.

45

WAR ON WEEDS

In small fields, farmers may be able to cut out every weed by hand. But on some big farms, farmers machine till the soil every spring before planting and every fall after harvesting their crops. The spring **tillage** kills the weeds that compete with crops for space, nutrients, and water. In the fall, farmers till to bury the remains of their harvested crops. This action exposes the soil so it will warm up faster for planting in the spring.

In some areas, such as in Africa and Asia, farmers till their small plots of land with plows pulled by animals. But modern methods of tillage are hard on the soil. Machine plowing, for example, exposes bare soil to erosion. Heavy tractors pack down the soil, making it difficult for water and air to enter the soil and fill underground pores.

Some U.S. farmers wondered what would happen if they stopped tilling so much. Less tilling might protect the soil.

On large farms, heavy equipment is needed to turn and break up the soil.

Many U.S. growers are introducing new farming techniques, including residue management. In the fall, after harvesting their corn crop, they leave the residue (roots and stalks) in the field. When snow and rain arrive in winter, the residue helps to hold in moisture so it does not drain from the land. Homeowners practice this idea when they leave grass clippings on their freshly mowed lawns.

But would the weeds take over? Would crop yields (amounts) go down?

As a test, some corn farmers did not plow the soil when the harvest was over. After gathering the corn, they left the **crop residue**—the roots and short stalks of corn—laying in the field. Like hands holding the soil, the crop residue helped to stop erosion. By not plowing, farmers prevented the weed seeds from taking root in the soil.

These practices are part of a new system of farming called **residue management.** It combines two ideas—tilling less and leaving crop residue in the field to protect the soil.

In most cases, the new farmers have found that residue management does not cause crop yields to go down, but it does reduce operating costs. By driving their equipment less, farmers save money on fuel and machine repairs and do not pack down the soil so much. In addition, scientists believe that the widespread use of residue management can decrease soil erosion by 90 percent.

A worker on an Israeli kibbutz (a self-sufficient farming community) examines plants watered by drip irrigation.

DRIP IRRIGATION

Water is scarce in Israel, a small country in the Middle East. The region's hot, dry climate encourages Israeli farmers to find efficient ways to irrigate their crops. One of these methods is **drip irrigation,** which involves the use of plastic pipes full of tiny holes.

Israeli farmers lay the pipes near the roots of plants. Water, often combined with nutrients, is pumped through the pipes and then slowly trickles down to the roots. Drip irrigation also allows farmers to control the timing and amount of water very carefully.

Most traditional types of irrigation—flooding, center pivot, and furrow—waste water. A lot of floodwater evaporates before it reaches the roots. Drip irrigation saves water, and smaller amounts have less chance to evaporate. Because only small amounts of water slowly and carefully drip from the pipes, the water does not leach minerals and nutrients. Nor does the water clog the soil's pores and hamper the flow of air.

MANAGING PESTS

For thousands of years, farmers have tried to get rid of insects and weeds that damage crops. Since the 1950s, most farmers have used expensive pesticides to kill insects and weeds. Although the chemicals eliminate unwanted pests, they can also harm soil, water, people, and wildlife. In the soil, for instance, insecticides and herbicides poison the billions of microorganisms that keep the soil healthy.

Farmers around the world are worried about the effects of chemicals on their soil and crops. In addition, they want to save money by using fewer costly insecticides and herbicides. One of the newest ideas is **integrated pest management,** often called IPM for short. It combines (integrates) several ways of controlling harmful insects and weeds using fewer or no chemicals.

When farmers walk through their fields, they can look for signs of pest and weed damage before applying any chemicals. This method, called IPM scouting, allows farmers to decide if insecticides and herbicides are needed and how much of them to apply. Another IPM technique stops outbreaks of pests by rotating (changing) crops. This practice interrupts the insects' growth cycle and prevents diseases caused by pests from starting.

The western corn rootworm, for example, is a corn pest that lays its eggs in late summer. The **larvae**—the wormlike stage of young insects—hatch in the spring, just in time to feed on corn roots. A farmer using IPM switches from planting corn one year to some other crop the next year. By

Integrated pest management (IPM) helps farmers control harmful insects without necessarily using chemicals. Here, workers capture grasshoppers to estimate the population of the pest. With this information, farmers can react to the grasshopper problem before the insects are so numerous that they ruin crops.

rotating the crops, the farmer deprives the larvae of the food they need to develop into adult rootworms. In this way, the farmer has eliminated the rootworms without using any chemicals.

Integrated pest management also has changed the farmers' traditional views of insects. Many insects, such as ladybugs and parasitic wasps, work for the farmer by attacking and killing pest insects. Under a United Nations program, Indonesian farmers examine their soils and plants to see which insects might get rid of pests.

In another use of IPM, farmers in Africa have come up with smart ways to use plants to protect other plants. One of their natural pesticides is a mixture of chili peppers and soap. When applied to vegetable gardens, it wards off flies, aphids, caterpillars, and other unwanted insects.

(Left) **Western corn rootworms, which eat the roots of corn plants, lay their eggs only in cornfields. By rotating a corn crop with some other crop, farmers take away the rootworm's nesting place and food supply.** *(Right)* **In another IPM method, beneficial insects—such as ladybugs, which feed on harmful pests—are introduced to areas full of damaging aphids.**

TRUST YOUR NEIGHBOR

In the Dominican Republic, a hilly, Spanish-speaking nation in the Caribbean Sea, local farmers are spreading the word about the benefits of sustainable agriculture. Through a program called CREAR, which means "to create" in Spanish, farmers leave their villages to be trained in new agricultural methods. The new techniques not only protect the soil but also increase crop yields. The trainees then return to their towns and villages in the Dominican countryside to share this knowledge with their friends, families, and neighbors.

Unlike foreign agricultural agents or government farming officials, the trainees live in and understand local conditions. As a result, the CREAR farmers gain the trust of other farmers and coax them into trying sustainable agricultural methods. These include contour tillage, strip cropping, and natural ways to control pests and weeds.

By using CREAR practices, Dominican farmers have boosted their yields of food crops. The increased volume also allows farmers to sell their surplus crops at local markets. In addition, the success of CREAR methods has shown many young rural Dominicans—who often move to cities in search of jobs—that farming has a bright future in their country.

A graduate of the CREAR program (kneeling) teaches a trainee about staking plants to help them grow.

OLD IS NEW AGAIN

Archaeologists (people who study past cultures) have uncovered ancient farming methods that can help modern farmers. In Bolivia, for example, archaeologists learned from the Tiwanaku, a people who

Irrigation canals surround a raised plot of soil on which modern Bolivians grow potatoes. This way of cultivating food was first used by the ancient peoples of this South American nation.

lived in the Andes Mountains more than a thousand years ago. The climate in the Andes is difficult for crop growing, with hot, sunny days, bitterly cold nights, and infrequent rainfall. Archaeologists found that the Tiwanaku farmed by building raised beds of soil and using a system of irrigation canals.

Modern Bolivian farmers did not know about or use Tiwanaku farming practices. Instead, they planted their crops on the slopes of the Andes, where erosion is a constant problem and where the topsoil is thin and low in nutrients. Encouraged by the archaeologists, Bolivian farmers are trying the old Tiwanaku methods. In raised beds of rich soil, they are now growing larger amounts of potatoes, barley, oats, and onions.

DIG THIS!

Many farmers have adopted or reintroduced methods that protect the soil, including contour tillage, strip cropping, and terracing. On sloping land, farmers

Using a method known as contour tillage, a farmer plows across, instead of up and down, the slope of a hill to prevent soil erosion.

Strip cropping, another means of reducing erosion, alternates short and tall crops in the same field. From the air, this practice creates geometric patterns on farmland.

plow across, rather than up and down, the slope. This technique creates horizontal ridges that catch water, which would otherwise carry topsoil down the hill.

Strip cropping also prevents erosion. In Canada and the United States, farmers sow grasses or other close-growing plants in between rows of grain crops. The blades and roots of the thick grasses decrease evaporation and act as breaks against wind erosion and sedimentation. On hillsides, the grasses also reduce water erosion.

Terracing is a popular farming method in South America, Asia, and Africa, where farmers cut wide, flat beds on steep hillsides. The terraces, which look like broad stairways, make it possible to grow crops on otherwise unfarmable land. Terracing also prevents soil erosion by keeping rainwater from rushing down hillsides.

MANY VERSUS ONE

Perennial polyculture is a farming practice that mimics (copies) a natural prairie. The prairie is a polyculture—a mixture of many kinds of grasses and flowering plants. The prairie plants are perennial, meaning they grow back each season from their roots. The prairie plants protect the

Growers in the Philippines cut stairlike terraces in the hillsides to stop rainfall from eroding topsoil.

The rich soil of prairies nourishes many kinds of grasses and flowers. Prairies also offer living spaces and food to birdlife, rodents, and other animals.

soil from erosion, and, when they die, they add their nutrients to the soil. For these reasons, prairies have the richest soils on earth.

Modern farming is based on the planting and harvesting of one crop per field each year, a method known as **annual monoculture.** For instance, farmers grow corn or soybeans from new seeds every year.

Annual monoculture can be hard on the soil. To replace nutrients lost each year, farmers spread a lot of fertilizers. Insecticides and herbicides are added to kill insects and weeds. Farmers need expensive farm equipment to gather the crop, and harvesting packs down the soil so that air and water cannot easily enter.

Scientists are experimenting with perennial polyculture to develop new kinds of crops that will grow together in the same field. These experts hope to invent seeds that will produce large yields of grain and that will not have to be replanted at the beginning of each season. What these specialists learn may influence farming methods in the twenty-first century. If farmers can copy the prairie's polyculture, they will enrich the soil while saving money on fuel, seeds, and chemicals.

CHAPTER FIVE

SAVING THE SOIL

People have been depending on soil for thousands of years, and right now we are facing a challenge. Our planet has a limited amount of fertile land, but the world's population is constantly increasing. By the year 2000, we will have a billion more mouths to feed than we had in the early 1990s! But only one-quarter of the earth has fertile soils for growing crops, and that figure is not going to change.

How are we going to feed all these new people? Can we feed them without harming our planet's water, air, and soil? Everyone—farmers, soil scientists, politicians, students, and home gardeners—will have to work together to answer these questions.

In June 1992, a large number of people concerned about our environment met in Brazil at the Earth Summit. They discussed soil erosion, air pollution, global warming, and many other pressing problems. They did not talk much about the impact that one billion more people will have on our resources in the twenty-first century.

(Left) Laborers in China, a country with more than one billion people to feed, pick salad greens. (Above) Rapid rates of population growth are changing the appearance of urban areas around the world, such as São Paulo in Brazil, where tall buildings dot the skyline.

UNITED NATIONS CONFERENCE ON ENVIRONMENT AND DEVELOPMENT

Rio de Janeiro 3–14 June 1992

In 1992, the United Nations sponsored a meeting on environmental issues that was attended by leaders from many countries.

In part, the Earth Summit members did not discuss population growth because of economic and social differences among nations and among ethnic groups. Rich countries, for example, can teach their citizens about the effects of population increases and can offer safe, inexpensive ways to limit family sizes. In poor countries, however, these methods and information are harder to come by.

The summit confirmed that personal actions—from writing letters to buying groceries—can influence decisions and highlight global problems. As individuals, we can help to show the link between population increases and environmental pressures so that government officials are forced to discuss these issues.

THE SCIENCE CONNECTION

To feed our growing population, scientists are exploring ways to improve crop yields. The theory is that, if farmers could grow more food on less land, they would stop planting in poor soils. We could rest lands that erode easily or that are lacking soil nutrients. Some governments offer rewards, such as lower taxes, to farmers who stop planting on poor farmland.

Scientists are also hoping to change the chemical makeup of plants. If a new type of grain could produce its own nitrogen, farmers would not have to use so much nitrogen fertilizer in the soil. African farmers have also expanded our scientific knowledge. On limited budgets, they have developed natural pesticides that fight

Scientists and soil specialists help farmers in developing nations to learn new agricultural methods. Here, agents show a Uruguayan how to broaden his range of crops (left) and check the progress of an experimental species of yucca in the Dominican Republic (right).

Home gardeners, as well as large-scale farmers, can get rid of unwanted insects and weeds by using natural pesticides instead of dangerous chemicals. Here, a scientist sprays a natural insecticide called Bt on tomato plants. Because the solution is harmless to humans, she does not need to wear protective clothing.

pests using tobacco, wood ash, mint leaves, soap, and other materials.

Many scientists are learning that nature is the best judge of plant conditions. Every type of plant is designed to grow in a certain climate and soil. In turn, every plant protects the soil in which it thrives best. One way to restore the health of the soil is to put back the native vegetation that

too much farming, grazing, and mining have damaged.

IN OUR OWN BACKYARDS

Leaders at faraway meetings cannot tackle the world's problems alone. Solutions begin at home and in our neighborhoods. Here are things we all can do to save the soil.

TAKING CARE OF KENYA'S SOIL

Soil erosion by wind and water is the most pressing environmental issue in Kenya, where the rapidly growing population has reached 26 million citizens. The need to feed more people convinces the government to allow tree cutting, which creates more farmland. High population growth rates also pressure farmers to produce more crops.

These concerns inspired a Kenyan teacher named Wangari Maathai to take action. In 1977, she founded the Green Belt movement—a tree-planting project that seeks to combat soil erosion, to slow the spread of the desert, and to provide scarce firewood to families. Since the movement began, more than 50,000 Kenyans—mostly women farmers—have planted millions of trees that safeguard acres (hectares) of topsoil.

Green Belt members establish tree nurseries, where seedlings are nurtured until they can be planted. The members then give the trees to farmers and are paid for each tree that survives. The program has given Kenyan women a chance to earn small incomes outside their household and farming duties. The success of Maathai's plan has encouraged other African nations to set up similar programs.

Wangari Maathai (left) hands a member of the Green Belt movement a tree seedling for planting.

USE FEWER CHEMICALS ON LAWNS AND IN GARDENS. Every year, to achieve green grass, homeowners in the United States dump 67 million pounds (30 million kilograms) of toxic chemicals on their lawns. These chemicals, although they kill insects or fertilize the grass, can also harm soil, groundwater, wildlife, and pets. Encourage your family to have a chemical-free lawn or to spread only organic insecticides and herbicides. Leave the grass clippings on the lawn.

PLANT NATIVE TREES AND SHRUBS. Many native plants protect the soil they are designed to live in. Urge your family to plant trees and shrubs that really belong in your gardens and backyards. Visit your library to find out what types of plants are native to your town or ask the local garden club for information on growing native plants.

GROW YOUR OWN ORGANIC VEGETABLES. You can have a small garden in pots if you have a sunny balcony, deck, fire escape, or windowsill. Organic gardening is a wonderful way to learn the

In West Virginia, a family works together to plant onions.

To avoid paying for costly herbicides, laborers on this farm in Nicaragua weed by hand.

value of healthy soil. When we work in the soil, we learn about soil texture, nutrients, and humus. When we grow our own food without using chemical additives, we depend less on foods that are grown with chemicals. Organic foods often taste fresher, too!

EAT ORGANICALLY GROWN FOOD. Cultivated without using chemicals, organic food is sometimes more expensive than food raised with fertilizers and pesticides. If more people supported organic farming, however, the price of organic food would drop. When we buy organic food, we encourage farmers to grow crops without chemicals. Putting fewer chemicals on crops leads to healthier soil and water.

MAKE YOUR OWN SOIL BY COMPOSTING. Encourage your family to start a compost heap in the backyard. When mixed with soil, your raked leaves, grass clippings, and food waste will decompose and turn into rich soil. You can use this soil in your flower and vegetable gardens. Composting reduces garbage, too. Most garden centers have information on composting.

REDUCE, REUSE, RECYCLE, DO WITHOUT. By using fewer resources, we reduce the need to take more minerals out of the soil or to overplant or overgraze. If your school or community does not yet have a recycling program, ask a teacher or a parent to help you start one.

WATCH IT ROT!

Composting, which reduces organic matter into a mixture of soil and nutrients, can be the best thing that ever happened to a garden, a lawn, or a potted plant. But a successful compost heap is not just a pile of rotting vegetables and lawn clippings. The heap's work force—bacteria and other microorganisms—needs the right combination of food, moisture, heat, and air to breed and feed.

Almost anything that was once alive can be tossed into a compost heap, but some materials benefit the heap more than others. Pine needles, for example, contain a natural chemical that prevents plants from growing. Broccoli stalks, eggshells, and other once-living kitchen waste are better choices. A healthy compost heap needs a good variety of organic ingredients.

Bacteria breed best in damp, warm conditions. The heap needs to be watered but not so much that it becomes soggy. As the bacteria breed, they produce energy in the form of heat. To keep in the warmth so that bacteria will continue to breed, most compost heaps are in covered bins. The tops and walls of the bins prevent the heat from escaping.

The whole compost heap could fail if the bacteria do not get enough air. As a result, a major part of composting involves turning the heap with a pitchfork. Mixing the rotting matter every few days lets in air so the rising population of bacteria can continue their work.

Young gardeners inspect a community compost heap in New York City.

This small business in Egypt makes bricks by combining soil with water and then pouring the mixture into molds. As the mixture dries in the sun, it takes on the shape of the mold. Within a few days, the bricks are hard enough to remove from the mold and sell to customers.

◾ *HELP YOUR PARENTS TO DISPOSE OF HOUSEHOLD CHEMICALS PROPERLY.* Old paint, used car oil, and leftover cleaning fluids that we carelessly dump on or in the ground can damage the soil, as well as groundwater.

◾ *TAKE A NEW LOOK AT SOIL.* When you are outdoors, look at the different soils around you. Notice their color and how they feel. Educate your family and friends about the soil's central place in our complex environment and remind them that a healthy earth starts with healthy soil.

City dwellers can learn about soil from potted plants, rooftop gardens, and grassy playgrounds.

ALLIANCE FOR ENVIRONMENTAL EDUCATION
51 Main Street
Post Office Box 368
The Plains, Virginia 22171

NATIONAL WILDLIFE FEDERATION
1400 16th Street NW
Washington, D.C. 20036

THE NATURE CONSERVANCY
1815 North Lynn
Arlington, Virginia 22209

SOIL AND WATER CONSERVATION SOCIETY
7515 Northeast Ankeny Road
Ankeny, Iowa 50021

SOIL CONSERVATION SERVICE
U.S. Department of Agriculture
Post Office Box 2890
Washington, D.C. 20013

THE WILDERNESS SOCIETY
900 17th Street NW
Washington, D.C. 20006

Photo Acknowledgments

Photographs are used courtesy of: pp. 1, 10 (top and bottom), Steve Foley / IPS; p. 4, NASA; pp. 6, 29, 38 (top and bottom), 39, Christine Osborne Pictures; p. 7, Nigel Harvey; p. 8, Don & Pat Valenti / Root Resources; p. 9, © Raymond A. Mendez; p. 11 (left), Shmuel Thaler; p. 11 (right), Hans-Olaf Pfannkuch; p. 12 (left), David Chittenden; p. 12 (right), UNICEF; p. 13, James Blank / Root Resources; pp. 14, 20, 36, 47, 53 (right), Soil Conservation Service; pp. 15 (top and bottom), 16 (right), © Karelle Scharff; pp. 16 (left), 22, 23, 53 (left), 60, USDA; p. 17 (top), American Association of Petroleum Geologists; p. 17 (bottom), National Association of Conservation Districts; p. 18, Irish Tourist Board; p. 19 (left), Craig Bihrle, NDGF; p. 19 (right), The Hutchison Library; p. 24, AID; p. 25, © Rick Poley; p. 26-27, Westinghouse Hanford Company; pp. 28 (left), 30, 43, 45, 56, FAO; p. 28 (right), Phyllis Cerny; pp. 31 (left), 68 (top), Australian Tourist Commission; pp. 31 (right), 46, Morning Star Photo; p. 32, National Museum of African Art, Eliot Elisofon Archives, Smithsonian Institution; p. 33 (top), Thomas Spellman, Kentucky N.R.E.P.C.; p. 33 (bottom), Kay Shaw; p. 34, Library of Congress; p. 37, Oriental Institute of the University of Chicago; p. 40, Leonard Soroka; p. 41, Steve Brosnahan; p. 42, CIDA / Pierre St-Jacques; p. 44, Patrick Cone; p. 48, Nancy Durrell McKenna; pp. 49, 50 (left), ARS, USDA; p. 50 (right), © Kent Wood; p. 51, Mark Feedman / Rural Development Service Group; p. 52, © Wolfgang Schüler; p. 54, Philippine Department of Tourism; p. 55, Jim Rathert / Missouri Department of Conservation; p. 57, Jim Cron; pp. 58, 61, UN Photo; p. 59 (left), David Mangurian; pp. 59 (right), 63, Inter-American Development Bank; p. 62, © Thomas R. Fletcher; p. 64, © Richard B. Levine; p. 65 (left), Steve Feinstein; p. 65 (right), © Frances M. Roberts; p. 67 (left), EDR Media; p. 67 (right), Department of Regional Industrial Expansion; p. 68 (bottom), EPA; p. 69, Rick Hanson / Minnesota Department of Agriculture; p. 70, World Bank.

Front cover: U. S. Department of Agriculture
Back cover: (Left) © Andrew E. Beswick; (Back) Inter-American Development Bank

alluvium: material—including clay, silt, sand, gravel, and mud—that flowing water deposits in rivers, lakes, and valleys.

annual monoculture: a farming practice that raises one type of crop year after year in the same field.

bacteria (bak-TEER-ih-yah): groups of very small organisms (microorganisms) that eat living and dead material.

chemical weathering: the gradual breakdown of rocks into soil through exposure to certain chemicals.

An Iraqi grower weeds his crop, which thrives in a fertile, river-carried soil called alluvium.

Modern harvesting machines gather grain in Alberta, a province in western Canada.

crop residue (REHZ-ih-doo): the portion of a plant left in the field after harvesting.

debris (deh-BREE): the loose material made by the breakdown of plants and rocks.

decomposition: the breakdown of organic matter by bacteria.

desertification (dih-zert-uh-fuh-KAY-shun): the process of making or expanding deserts by overgrazing livestock, overplanting crops, or overcutting vegetation.

(Right) **Erosion by wind helped to shape the Olgas, large boulders that rise in central Australia.** *(Below)* **Studying samples of the soil will help this scientist determine if the groundwater has been polluted.**

drip irrigation: a direct, water-saving method of nourishing plants. Drip systems trickle water to plant roots from small holes in pipes.

erosion (ih-RO-zhun): the wearing away or washing away of soil by wind or water.

fertilizer: a chemical substance added to the soil that helps plants grow.

floodplain: a low, flat area next to a river or stream.

groundwater: water that is stored beneath the ground in the soil's pores.

herbicide: a chemical designed to kill unwanted plants, such as weeds.

humus (HYOO-muss): brown or black material made from rotted plants and animals that is the organic part of soil.

insecticide: a chemical designed to kill unwanted insects or bugs.

integrated pest management (IPM): the combination of several ways to contain and get rid of pests while reducing or stopping the use of pesticides.

irrigation: applying water to land for farming purposes.

larva: the wormlike stage of a recently hatched insect.

leaching: the removal from topsoil of nutrients and other beneficial substances by water that filters deep into the soil.

loess (LUSS): material moved and deposited by wind and made up mostly of silt-sized particles.

microorganism: a tiny life form not visible without the help of a microscope.

mineral: a natural, nonliving substance.

nutrient (NOO-tree-int): a substance used as food by plants or animals.

organic matter: dead plants and animals in the soil that are in various stages of rotting.

A farmer spreads liquid nitrogen fertilizer on his cornfield.

organism: any living thing.

parent material: the solid mineral from which a specific type of soil forms.

perennial polyculture: a farming practice that combines several kinds of plants in the same field. Each year, the plants grow back from their roots without needing reseeding.

pesticide (PES-tih-side): a chemical used to destroy pests.

physical weathering: the gradual breakdown of rocks through exposure to wind, water, or sun.

pore: a small space within soil that can hold water or air.

residue management: a farming method that leaves crop residue on a field to improve and protect the soil.

salination: the buildup of dissolved salts in the soil.

sedimentation: the buildup of solid materials, such as soil or organic matter, that water or air has moved from their original place to a new location.

strip mining: a mining process that strips away the upper layers of soil to reach deposits of minerals or fuels.

Using an earthenware container, an Ethiopian farmer carefully waters young trees.

sustainable agriculture: the use of land through careful farming practices to maintain continuous yields of crops without harming the soil, water, air, and other parts of nature.

tillage: using machines or tools to loosen and break up the soil for seeding, weeding, or other farming activities.

topsoil: the surface layer of soil in which plants grow.

INDEX